Glen More

a drive thro

Written and illustrated by
Jackie LeMay
With botanical notes and drawings by
Joanna Gardner

Brown & Whittaker
Reprinted 2003

Published by Brown & Whittaker Publishing
Tobermory PA75 6PR

Main text and illustrations © Jackie LeMay
Botanical text and illustrations © Joanna Gardner

ISBN 09532775 6 9

2001

Set in Times New Roman and printed in Tobermory, Scotland

Glen More

has been described in so many different ways and, even today, with a good tarmac road running through it, it has many moods. Travel through on a clear spring morning and it seems the most peaceful and beautiful place on earth, but come through when the clouds are low on the hills and the rain is lashing down and you may agree with Keats, writing in 1818 "the road through the island, or rather the track, is the most dreary you can think of, between dreary mountains, over bog and rock and river." Or even with Dr John MacCulloch writing in 1824 "Trackless and repulsive, rude without beauty, stormy, rainy, dreary." Or may, like me, agree with MacCormick in his book *The Island of Mull*, published in 1923, who wrote "one may possibly not encounter a fellow traveller on the lone road, but the picturesqueness of the region through which we are passing is so charming and so full of romance that the solitude is an accentuating attribute to the wild grandeur of the scene."

There is very little known about the early history of the glen. The only standing stones and the hill fort recorded in this area are outside the actual glen although the impressive hill fort at Ardvergnish stands on guard at the west end. It occupies the summit of a rocky boss looking down on the remains of the early settlement and the present farm below. With its ring of tumble and spectacular backdrop of Ben More, it is a wonderfully atmospheric place.

The first map to show a road through the glen is Thomson's *Atlas* of 1824, but well before this, the hills were criss-crossed with tracks and drove roads and there were settlements through most of its length. Today, as you journey through the glen, you pass only two roofed houses and one or two ruins that can be clearly seen, but there are many more to discover. I have given the four most convenient stopping places, but the whole length of the road is a journey of discovery.

Dugald MacPhail memorial

Stop first where you enter the glen at the junction with the road to Lochbuie and Croggan. Here, a section of the old road leads off to the left just before the cattle grid, down to a convenient parking place. A little way back on a rocky knoll above the road, you will see the memorial to Dugald MacPhail (1818-1877) "the roadmaker", Mull's great bard. The monument, built in 1920 from stones said to be those of his former house, has a verse of his best known poem "An t-Eilean Muileach" inscribed on each of the four sides. The first verse is Mull's anthem and sung at the end of many a social event and ceilidh.

An t-Eilean Muileach, an t-eilean aghmhor,
An t-Eilean grianach mu'n iath an saile,
Eilean buadhmhor nam fuar bheann arda,
Nan coilltean uaine, 's cluaintean fasail

The Isle of Mull of isles the fairest
Of ocean's gems the first and rarest:
Green grassy isle of sparkling fountains
Of dark green woods and tow'ring mountains

He wrote it, like so many Gaelic poems, when
he was far from his native land, working as an
architect in Newcastle. He came back, it is
said, to Mull to have his children educated and
lived here at Strathcoil. The foundations of a
house just a little beyond the monument may
well have been Dugald's own from which the
monument was built. Other remnants of the
abandoned village of Strathcoil are hidden in
the forestry plantation across the road.

If you return to the parking place and walk along the old road by the River
Lussa, you will come to the memorial of John Jones, who died on the 1st
April 1891, from smallpox which was rife at this time. This is a sad story.
John Jones, the pedlar, going on his rounds in the Ross of Mull found two
families riddled with smallpox. Shunned by their neighbours, they had no one
to draw water for them or look after their basic needs so the pedlar went to the
rescue and nursed them through the worst of their illness. When he resumed
his journey, his pack on his back, he found that he had caught the disease and
with no one to nurse him, he died by the roadside where the cairn now stands.

Drive on up the present main road and a little further on, beyond the forestry
enclosure look across the river to the left to the settlement called Arinasliseig.
The last house here to be inhabited, although only a ruin now, stands out
clearly on a little plain close to the river bank. Above, on the hillside and
close by there are traces of several other buildings.

There is a sad story told about one of the last families to live here at the turn
of the nineteenth century. They were a family called Boyd, cousins of the
MacGillivrays of Burg. Nine of them died of consumption (tuberculosis) and
only one son survived and he was remembered for being phenomenally
strong.

Another story about this house is the reason for its name – The house of the
slicing. There are many versions this story, but basically the family living
here sheltered the baby who was the rightful heir to the Lochbuie lands and
were "sliced down" one by one, defending his hiding place.

Torness

From here, it is only a short way on to the ruins of Torness, which is another convenient stopping place with things of interest to see. About a quarter of a mile before the big bend in the road, you will see on the left the substantial remains of an old barn. You can come off here to park on another useful section of the old road. Very little remains of the farmhouse, which is on the other side of the road a little further back and was lived in until the 1930s. The main route through Glen Forsa started here. Sadly, the path, which was still quite easy to follow comparatively recently, has disappeared with the forestry planting although a branch of the same path, which runs round the foot of Ben Talaidh can still be discovered in part.

The barn and the fank on the other side of the road are clearer to see. A market, possibly only for horses, was held at Torness annually in August. There is an interesting note in the "Minutes of the Commissioners of Supply, for the Northern District of Argyll" dated 28th March 1826: "Mr Campbell, factor for Colonel Campbell of Possil, produced a Petition, complaining of the injury sustained by the Farm of Torness on account of the Horse Market being annually held on that farm without remuneration being allowed therefore." The cattle and horse markets were eventually moved to a permanent site at Balemeanach (Fishnish) given by Lochbuie. Just below the barn and fank, where the ground slopes down to the river, can be traced the market stances (whether these were benches for sales goods or sleeping bothies, opinions differ). At least eight can be found. To find these stances, follow the path that leads down to the bridge over the river and stop at a cairn. Nearby, you should find rectangular outlines of stone foundations about a foot high and measuring 8-10 feet long and 4-5 feet wide. At the time of the fair, branches and heather would be gathered to form temporary roofs.

There is a fascinating map of 1787 of this area, showing five ways from the head of Glen Forsa. It is entitled "Plan and Measurement of the situation of three places of worship in the parish of Torrosay, Mull." It shows a criss-cross of paths going in all directions to destinations as far apart as Inegard (by Carsaig), Iona, Salen and Knock. It was here that Sarah Murray, writing in 1799, indefatigable traveller as she was, nearly got lost. She writes "I journeyed many miles thro' this Alpine scenery, till I came to a diminutive plain, with three tracks from different glens leading to it." Here they took the wrong path and climbed the zig-zag ascent to Mam Bhradhadail. "It was one of the hottest days I ever felt," she writes, "and the labour of scrambling up the steep road among loose stones for two miles was dreadful. When I reached the summit of the hill, I exclaimed 'Dugall, we are wrong! How shall we get back down that dreadful zig-zag?' In certain lights you can see the zig zag at the top of the pass, just to the left of the line of the burn. Mrs Murray and Dugall did get down safely somewhere further along the ridge near Ishriff. She continued: "we descended to a glen, in which is a small lake and a hut or two at the end of it." They were told they were on the right track for Pennycross. "Other burns and rough passes were to be surmounted; at last we came to a spot from which two tracks branched; one I believe leads to Moy at the head of Loch Buy [this may well have been the path which is still open today, leading down by the lochans to Lochbuie]. The other to the head of Loch Scridain."

There are stories told of the people from Glen Cannel carrying their sacks of corn over this hill pass (Mam Bhradhadail) to the mill at Lochdon. On many estates the tenants were forced to take their corn to be ground at the estate mill. This was called "thirlage" and had the dual purpose of raising revenue and giving the landlord added control over his tenants. At the same time, the small "click-mills" and hand-querns were outlawed in many areas.

Ewan of the Little Head

Driving along from Torness it is not long before Loch Sguabain comes into sight.

During the middle ages, we see the beginning of the clan system and the clan chiefs living like minor kings in their own territories. To this period belongs the structure on the island in Loch Sguabain. The island is traditionally associated with "Eoghain a Chin Bhig," Ewan of the Little Head, a son of John MacLean, 5th Lord of Loch Buie. At some time, it has been fortified by a massive dry-stone perimeter wall. Munro, writing in 1549, describes it as "an inhabited strength." So presumably Ewan fortified it or added to its fortifications, maybe when he fell out with his father, which led to his death, when he fought against him and was decapitated in the battle. From this comes the story of the ghost of the Headless Horseman. Any evening at dusk, you may meet the decapitated rider, galloping down the glen, and he is said to gallop furiously round Moy Castle, when there is a death in the MacLaine family. After the battle, their leader dead, the

routed clan fled on down the glen towards Loch Scridain, but they did not escape. They got no further than the small flattish plain just above Craig. Here they were virtually wiped out. They are said to be buried by the burn named Allt Clan Iain, to the west of Arighloire, which is marked on some older maps.

On the shores of Loch Sguabain, near the restored house and barn of Ishriff there are the footings of earlier houses and on the slope above the loch, there are the foundations of several more buildings. Up the glen to the right of the main road, are the remains of the houses of Clachvule, which is still marked on the map. Further up the same glen, Glen Molach, are several interesting sheiling sites. Above the loch named after the giant Sguabain, on a corner of the old road, sits a pointed stone, Clach Sguabain. The story goes as follows: two Fingalain giants, Nichol and Sguabain had a heated argument. One giant was standing by Loch Spelve and the other here above this loch. They were so tall they could see each other over the hills. They got so angry that Sguabain picked up a huge rock and hurled it at Nichol who, in return, threw this great pointed rock at Sguabain and it has sat here above the loch ever since.

The Three Roads

As you come to the highest point in the glen above the string of lochs, ahead on the left of the modern road, about 200 feet up on the shoulder of the hill is the earliest recorded road through the glen, called locally the

8

"Drove Road," and built, I was told, at this height to avoid the snow drifts which often blocked the pass below. Near here it forked, one branch going left above the lochans towards Lochbuie and the other crossing a small burn and climbing along the hillside.

Just below the fork, on the slope, is "The Priest's Well", Tobar Leac an t'Sagairt, and to this belongs a very sinister story. Two priests from Iona were racing against each other to take possession of the living of Killean. Having raced up the steep part of the drove road, the leader stopped for a drink at the well. The other one coming up behind, murdered him as he stooped to drink and went on to take the parish.

At this point, three generations of the road are quite visible as shown in the drawing: the drove road, the old tarmac road and the modern road. The old road swings to the right and follows the curve of the hills. If you look care-fully at the old road, you can pick out Arighloire with an old fank and signs of a house. Here the second of the main passes from the north comes into the glen. This is the Harp Pass, Mam an Tiompain, and to this pass belongs another sad story. There are many versions, but one of the best known is this: Neil MacLean of Lochbuie had a childhood friend, Barabel, the daughter of his old nurse. Neil goes to France to finish his education and

Barabel goes home and is betrothed to a celebrated harpist. Before their marriage, they decide to visit the village where they are to live. On the way home, they get caught in a snow storm. Barabel is frozen and loses consciousness. The harpist does all he can to keep her warm, finally chopping up his precious harp to burn. She revives and, just at that moment, Neil, who had been hunting with his men nearby, sees the fire and comes over. Barabel and Neil recognise each other, but do not let on to the Harpist. When the storm abates, they all set out together. Later, complaining of a great thirst, Barabel gives her fiancé the slip while he goes to find her water, and runs off with Neil, deserting her betrothed. From this comes the Gaelic saying "she is not worth burning your harp for."

The drove road on the far side of the pass is a little difficult to pick out, but as you descend, you will see a large, square-shaped rock, used as a marker and known by the name Creag Mholach, or "the stone with the hair on top," presumably because of the growth of heather on the top. If you look down the glen, following the line of the river, you will see another conspicuous stone, oval in shape, also thought to have been a marker for the drove road, but also said to have been one of the boundary stones between the Kingdom of the Picts and the Kingdom of Dalriada. Here the drove road would appear to join the same route as the old tarmac road.

The old road crosses the river just above Craig, where there was at least one more house on the other side as well as the present house. From here it curved round under the hills to the farm of Derrynaculen and so down to Kinloch.

Holly Tree Fank

At the western end of the glen, there were several routes coming over the hills, linking the north of the island with the south. A good place to appreciate these is at the holly tree fank at Teanga Brideig, where the modern road sweeps to the right of the glen and where there is an attractive old bridge. The main route over Mam Clachaig joins the road here but further up there were two less well defined routes over Mam Tiumpail and Mam Choireadail. The

middle route is known locally as "Columba's Way." This, I was told, was for "important people" and was paved. Certainly some of the stone edging and paving slate can still be found on the upper hillside, and at the top of the pass, marked by a cairn, is Columba's Well - but how it got its name and its "important" status no one seems to know.

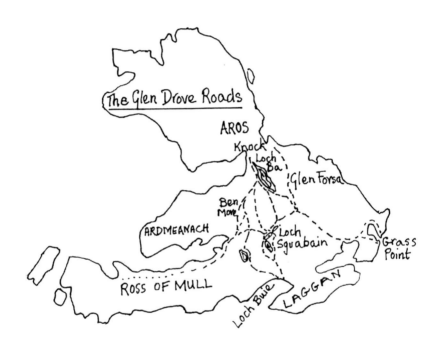

The third route from Mam Coireadail has a very steep way down to the houses at Craig and marked at the top here is a well called by the same name as the pass, Tobar Choireadail, but this is difficult to find. It is a stiff climb up, but coming from Craig it is the shortest way into Glen Cannel and I was told it was regularly used.

From the bottom of the Mam path, at the Holly Tree Fank, the way went over the present road and along by the river to Derrynaculen. A branch to the right, over the ford, led through rather swampy ground to Torbreck, where a path led out to the head of Loch Scridain. At one time, this house was said to be a collecting or sorting point for post coming over the Mam from Salen.

If you want to see an interesting sheiling site, climb up the Mam Clachaig path for about 200 feet and you will find several hut sites to the right of the path.

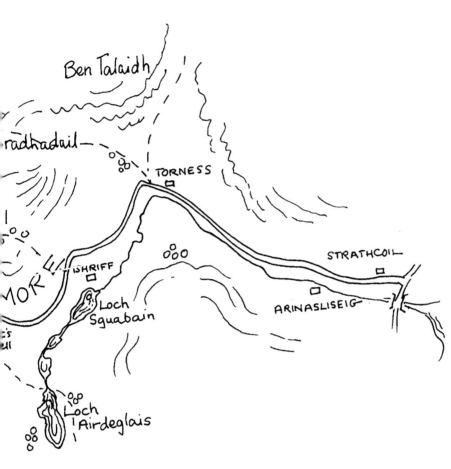

Ben Talaidh

radhadail

TORNESS

ISHRIFF

STRATHCOIL

MOR

Loch
Squabain

ARINASLISEIG

Loch
Airdeglais

$\begin{smallmatrix} O O O \\ O O \end{smallmatrix}$ = explored
sheiling sites

The Road in History

The Glen road was specified in the "Argyllshire Road Acts of 1800" as one of the "great lines to be preferred," meaning the route was to be give priority by the Mull District Road Trustees along with the other "great lines from Achnacraig to Tobermory." The next Act of 1816 does not mention "great lines" anywhere. The minutes of the District Road Trustees have a few references to "sporadic work" in Glen More before 1825, but that year they resolved that a road from Clachandow in Torosay to Fionnphort "is to be commenced in the course of next spring." A Glenmore Road Committee was appointed to manage the project and presumably work went ahead.

The Duke of Argyll had been writing for several years asking for a road from Bunessan to Loch Don to facilitate the movement of cattle from Coll, Tiree and the Ross of Mull to Loch Don, where they were shipped to the mainland. We find James Hope, acting for the Commissioners, writing in 1812 "I should not be much surprised if there were still a blow up . . ." Or did he mean a hold up?

It was not plain sailing. Even in the 1850s there was still trouble. A list of claims against the Trustees include "To damage sustained by horses and carts in consequence of these roads not being kept in repair by the Road Trustees." Later in the same year, 1853, there is a claim by a Mr Cumstie of Tobermory for £4..5/- "being the alleged price of a horse, said to be killed in consequence of a hole in the Glen More road."

There is an Act of Parliament of 1669 in which the landowners were told "to convene all tenants and coatters and their servants . . . to have in readiness horses, carts, fleeds (sledges), spades, shovels, picks, mattocks and such other instruments as shall be required for the repair of the said highways . . .the days not to exceed "six days for man and horse yearlie for the first three years and four days yearlie thereafter." They were to be paid.

At the turn of the nineteenth century, this law was still in force, but by 1852, when there was a spate of letters complaining about the state of the roads again, "statute labour" had been abolished and the roads were to be maintained by tax and tenantry responsibility and were now called "Parish Roads". Several tacksmen and landowners at this time felt that the Mull District Road Trustees were not doing their share, but the Trustees complained that the tax levied so little money that they could not afford the bridges and general upkeep they were meant to provide. We do find, in contemporary documents, that they paid for making a "new Bridle Path over Glen Clachaig hill" which had been "entirely neglected for the last five years and was almost impassable with a horse."

The Runner (postman) was still crossing this way at the end of the nineteenth century, bringing the post from Salen over the Mam and down to Kinloch where he exchanged post with the Bunessan postman, both men doing a round trip of thirty miles or more.

The complaints go on about the dangerous state of the Glen road, mostly to do with the mail. "The mounted messenger who travels the road in question, has more than once lately, not only been unable to proceed on his journey but has incurred considerable risk of his life . . . three bridges would make all the difference." This in December 1882. The following January, there is a letter from the Surveyor General saying that bridges would not be the right answer, but rather "inverted arches" which appear to be paved fords through the burns. "The streams over which you proposed we should make bridges are nothing in the summer or dry weather but in winter they are occasionally torrents bringing down stones and gravel which would choke and eventually carry away bridges and matters would be worse than ever. Inverted arches with paved bottoms as at present existing in Glen More are far better." And, of course, much cheaper! The same writer goes on "most days the mail cart is the only conveyance that passes." So he suggests "let the Bunessan and Kinloch Scridain mails go to Salen by steamer and your runner work between Bunessan and Salen over the so called Gribun road. It is a mile or two longer but the road is good, with more traffic on it and more inhabitants to serve on the road and so avoid Glen More where there are none." Today the Glen road is a far safer road than the Gribun road which, in the wet months is often "bombed" with stones from the cliffs above.

The Sheilings

It is difficult to date the old village settlements but what is certain with the introduction of sheep and the people turned off the land, many of their houses were demolished and the stones used to build fanks. As you travel through the glen, you pass at least seven fanks, some like that at Derrynaculen with the shearing benches still showing clearly. With the smallholdings of the people amalgamated into bigger farms and sheepwalks, often only one shepherd lived in an area which before had supported several families and as the shepherds and their sheep took over the hill pastures so the sheiling settlements went out of use and a whole way of life was lost.

Many of the sheiling sites can still be found. In our area the huts were mostly of round construction. The settlements can often be located by the rashes of good green grass still around them. Here the women would bring the cattle and the few house sheep for the summer months for better

grazing and to keep the animals away from the cultivated areas round the townships. While there, they would make butter and cheese, which often went in part rent for their farms. According to some accounts it was almost like a summer holiday away from the smoke and the mud of their crowded settlements . . . and possibly even from their menfolk!

In some areas, the men would go up to the hills ahead of the women and rebuild the previous year's huts, possibly finishing the walls with turf and covering the roof with heather. It is thought that small timbers for the roofs and a wattle door would have been carried up from the home farm. When all was ready, the men would return to the farm below and the women would travel up with their animals, taking their churns and milking pails, dishes and skimmers, hobbles for the cows and anything else they needed for the summer weeks.

Contact was usually kept with the home farm, in some places the women went home in the morning and came back in the evening with food for both humans and animals. Sometimes the visit was just once a week, sometimes not at all. It has been said that there was often plenty to subsidise food at the sheilings: milk and all its products, blackberries, crowberries, birds' eggs and even the occasional trout from the streams.

Osgood Mackenzie, writing in *A Hundred Years in the Highlands* describes life at the sheilings. He gives a graphic account of butter-making: "the girls were in the habit of finding just sufficient room behind their heads for the big wooden receptacle which held all the week's supply of cream. So that it might ripen sooner from the warmth of their bodies and turn more quickly into butter in the churn.

As you travel through the Glen, most of the sites are above you on the hillsides, but one that can fairly easily be found is in the valley below the footpath to Mam Bhradhadail. Here seven or eight round huts show quite clearly. Another site that is easy to find is at Teanga Brideig on the footpath to Mam Clachaig. Here the huts are slightly bigger and oval in shape. Many still retain three or four courses of stones. Some have a small building attached, which would have served as a dairy and in some, if you look carefully, you may find a built-in shelf or keepy hole.

The Clearances

The population of the island peaked in 1821 at 10,612, a number which included soldiers returning from the Napoleonic wars. The land could not support these sorts of numbers and in many areas the people were subsisting on potatoes and when the potato blight struck in the middle years of the century, the situation became desperate. At the same time, the trade in black cattle slumped badly, the preference in the markets now being for stall-fed lowland breeds, so the crofters lost about the only monetary income they had, their purchasing power to buy meal or pay rents.

Meanwhile the landowners were under severe economic pressure. Their lifestyle had changed and many were now absentee landlords with town houses and other estates to maintain. There was no way the indigenous population could pay the rents the landlords now demanded and to let the land as sheepfarms ensured a stable return, so the people had to go. Most estates on Mull were under sheep by the 1840s according to "Destitute Papers, First Report of the Central Relief Board, 1847," and the people cleared from the land.

Much has been written about the clearances and there are horrifying stories of the people being burnt out of their houses, but little is known that actually happened in the Glen settlements. We do know that not all the Mull landowners were uncaring.

Some tried re-settlement programmes and others paid for passages to Canada and America, but we find in the censuses for the second half of the century that the only houses still lived in in the Glen are those occupied by shepherds and their families. These are at Arinasliseig, Torness, Ishriff, Craig and Torbreck. Derrynaculen is not mentioned.

The following letter is sadly typical. Richard Somers, writing in 1847, as a result of his *Tour of Inquiry in the Highlands* gives us a graphic and disturbing account of four families ejected from the farms of Ardvergnish. Two of these had taken refuge in Tobermory. "I went to see them." They had taken two empty rooms in the upper flat of a back house. In one of the families there were ten children, several of whom were in the room when I entered. The mother, a woman of very respectable appearance was making thin porridge for their supper; they had got a similar meal in the morning; and this was their whole diet. The rooms were very bare of furniture, containing only a few things which they had carried over the mountains. The farm on which these families lived as cottars was let at Whitsunday, soon after which time they were ejected, and their cottages pulled to the ground.

For six weeks they lived in a tent during the day, but as many as could be accommodated were provided with beds by neighbours at night. The cold of winter, however, at length drove them out . . . Both men at the time of my visit were absent at the herring fishing. As soon as they had seen their families safely housed they had trudged away back to Kilfinichen, to make the most of the fishing season, which had been so rudely and cruelly interrupted by their ejectment."

The last inhabitants

Of the shepherds living in the cottages through the Glen at the turn of the century some worked for the Torosay estate, some for Glen Forsa and one for Lochbuie. George MacRae and his family lived in the cottage across the river at Craig. There was a bridge across just above the cottages, the stone piers for it are still visible but the support in the middle of the river has long since been washed away and the cottage pulled down. MacRea worked for Lochbuie and would walk through the hills by Loch Fuaran to the farm, but his son assured me that he did not have to go every day. When they were gath-

ering sheep, it was a twelve mile drive through the Glen to the home farm, a long walk for both sheep and shepherd. Both the Craig cottages had good crofts. The MacRaes had good fields and a large vegetable garden. They kept two cows and some pigs.

School for all the children living in the glen was quite a problem. There seems to have been "school" in various places at various times. At one time at Ishriff, another at Craig and another at Ardvergnish. In the thirties, the children from the two cottages at Craig walked down to the Holly Tree Fank, where the farmer from Derrynaculen kept his car. He gave them a lift to Kinloch from where they had to walk on to the school house at Pennyghael. The younger ones had their lessons at Ardvergnish. It was too far for them to walk to Pennyghael, but it is not recorded who taught them. One child who lived at Torness had to go to school at Lochbuie where she was a weekly boarder. On a Monday morning she would walk down the glen to Ardura bridge, where she was picked up in a pony and trap and driven down to Lochbuie. There she stayed for the week, returning the same way on a Friday afternoon. Walking never seems to have been much of a problem. The young people from Craig and Derrynaculen thought nothing of walking over the hills to Carsaig for the dances, which seemed always to have been very popular there. They worked hard but they played hard too.

Now the hills are mostly empty: just a few sheep, deer and walkers but there is one brave new house at Ishriff accompanied by its refurbished barn. Maybe this signals the re-awakening of the glen.

NATURAL HISTORY

In the old days, most of the Glen lay within the parish of Torosay and the "Statistical Account 1791-1799" gives us a fascinating insight into what it was like, "The general surface of the Parish of Torosay is mountainous, and these mountains are mostly covered with heath. . . some of these mountains are excellent sheepwalks, and others are very barren. From the top of the mountain called Ben More or the Great Mountain, most of the Western Isles may, with a clear sky, be seen at one view, as distinctly as if they were laid down upon a sheet of paper. Bentaluidh also, or Prospect Mountain as the word seems to import, commands a very extensive view on all sides, and sailors give it the name of the Sugar Loaf" The account goes on to say: "In the mountains of Torosay there are red deer, foxes, eagles, hawks, grouse, blackcock, tarmagan and, in the winter, woodcocks." There are some woods in the lower part of the Glen "mostly birch, with some oak and ash. These woods are occasionally sold for charcoal to the Lorn Furnace Company [at Taynuilt, near Oban]." Which may account for there being so few trees now.

In the report for the parish of Kilfinichen and Kilviceuen, in the same volume it is reported: "the only wild quadrupeds in the parish are deer, foxes and rabbits. The rabbits may be called strangers, having first appeared within these few years. The deer have always been natives . . . there is all the variety of land birds found in the parish that are generally met with in other parts of the highlands, such as eagles, hawks, kites, wild geese, pigeons, moorfowls, blackcocks, tarmagens etc etc."

As you travel through today, you may well see many of the same species, golden eagles, white-tailed eagles, hen harrier, short-eared owl, buzzard, sparrow-hawk, peregrine and the occasional merlin and if you climb some of the slopes, you may well see ptarmigan and grouse. These are all regularly recorded.

There are no foxes on Mull now but at one time they were a serious menace to farmers. In another fascinating report on the islands by the Rev Dr. John Walker of 1764 and 1771, he writes "the Devastations made among the sheep by the Eagles, but especially by the Fox is the great cause of their [sheep] high value in the Isle of Mull . . . This destructive Animal prevails so much that no farmer can pretend to keep more sheep that what he is capable of housing, as it is exposing them to certain Destruction to suffer them to ly abroad . . ."

Seton Gordon, writing in 1920, said that there were no foxes on Mull, though he had heard that "a couple of hundred years ago he (the fox) seems to have lived on the island."

Of the small animals, many seem to have been introduced. J.P. MacLean in his book *The History of the Island of Mull*, published in 1925 writes "in Mull the so-called Irish Hare (L. Hibernicus) occurs and was introduced at Loch Beg. The rabbit was introduced a short time before the *Old Statistical Account* was published in the 1790s. The mole was brought to Mull about the year 1808 by a vessel from Morvern that discharged an earthen ballast near Tobermory and had become quite numerous all over the island. The viper or adder in Mull is particularly large and venomous."

At the present time mink, said to have originally escaped from fur farms, cause a lot of damage to ground-nesting birds and can sometimes be seen in the glen.

The Flowers of Glen More by Joanna Gardner

Today in Glen More we see wide open hillsides, covered in Purple Moor-grass (Molinia caerulea), tussocky, difficult to walk on, and smothering all but the most persistent flowering plants. Few beasts will graze this tough grass, though sheep and deer nibble the young shoots through the winter. There are small lawns of closely cropped turf, and roadsides that provide a little grazing throughout the year. It is here, and in ravines inaccessible to sheep, that the wild flowers grow. There is little real woodland, apart from the forestry plantations. Much of the low ground is poor and boggy.

During the period between the sixteenth and the nineteenth century it must have been these lawns, then more extensive, that supported the sheilings. In those days, the lower slopes of the hills from Ben More to Ben Tallaidh probably carried woodland, birch, rowan, oak, ash and willow, the trees in the ravines extending well beyond their present limits . The population peaked at the beginning of the nineteenth century, and the increased demand for timber for building and fuel, for there was little peat, led to extensive felling. Then came the clearances and the introduction of large numbers of sheep. The practice of muirburn, burning off the heather to provide young growth for grazing, destroyed not only the seedling trees, but where pursued without care, destroyed much of the heather as well, encouraging the proliferation of the moorgrass. "Sheep, whose multitudinous feet did far more damage than the black cattle formerly farmed by the crofters, completed the rout of the timber" (Jermy and Crabbe, *Island of Mull*).

I have not attempted to list all the plants you can find, merely to follow the ancient roadways to the dwelling places of the early farmers, and the modern road through the Glen, and to point out some of the flowers that they would have seen and you can still find.

At Winter's end the hills are lion-coloured beneath the cold grey skies. The Moor Grass is dead, coming away readily if pulled, and blown in drifts across the road. Within living memory this "White Grass" was gathered and used to stuff palliases until they were a metre thick. This provided a soft bed that was squashed thinner and thinner until renewed each Spring. We begin our journey at Ardura in the Spring. Here there are modern conifer plantations, but one can still see the quite extensive oak woodland, around, and to the south, of the River Lussa. There are many brooding holly trees. In some places these were planted as waymarkers, their dark evergreen foliage standing out against misty or snow covered hillsides. Whether this was so here I know not, but you will certainly find isolated holly trees high in the hills. At Teanga Brideig, where the pass over Creag Mhic Fhionnlaidh meets the road, there is a splendid old holly that must have been a good landmark for those descending in bad weather.

In the patches of woodland are Primroses (Primula vulgaris), Wood Sorrel, Oxalis acetosella), and Wood Anemones (Anemone nemorosa). Hidden in the shelter of tussocks are the little Dog Violets (Viola riviniana). There is Wood Sage (Teucrium scorodonia), with its pale greenish-yellow flowers and wrinkly leaves. Hazels, formerly coppiced to provide timber for building and hurdles, are hung with pale yellow catkins. This tree was associated in Celtic mythology with fire and fertility. Bluebells (Hyacinthoides non-scripta) colour the hillsides in May. All of this group of plants also flourish in some places on the open hillside, indicators that the woodlands were once more extensive.

WOOD SAGE

The farmer at Arinasliseig (the House of the Slicings) may have struggled to grow a few crops, probably bere (and inferior type of barley), oats and potatoes. Here nettles (Urtica dioica) and docks (Rumex obtusifolius) would have flourished in the extensive middens. These plants often remain as indicators of human habitation long after buildings have vanished beneath the grass. There is little to be seen just here of nettles and docks now, but they are still common in various other places through the glen. As is Silver Weed (Potentilla anserina). In times of hardship the roots of this beautiful plant, with its feathery silver-grey leaves and acid yellow flowers, were harvested and ground into a sort of crude flour. Pignut (Conopodium majus) grows here too. This dainty little plant of the cow parsley family has small brown tubers that were dug for food, and are still relished by children who know of their existence.

In summer the young women left the farms, to take their cattle up to the sheilings on the high hillsides. And we can walk as they did to the place where the five roads meet. The roadsides, where the grass is short and sweet for the sheep, are bright with yellow flowers. Birdsfoot Trefoil (Lotus corniculatus), Tormentil (Potentilla erecta), Slender, or perhaps more correctly Beautiful, St Johns Wort (Hypericum pulchrum) and Lady's Bedstraw, (Galium verum), together with its white-flowered cousin Heath Bedstraw (Galium Saxatile), grow here. Hidden in the grass are the bright blue flowers of the little Heath Milkwort (Polygala serpyllifolium) and Purple Thyme (Thymus drucei). There are several representatives of the large family of eyebrights (Euphrasia sp), and if you look closely their

25

seemingly insignificant white flowers are often full of colour, pink and violet, with touches of yellow.

Cotton Grass (Eriophorum angustifolium) blows in the wind warning of the presence of boggy ground; as does its cousin Hares Tail (Eriophorum vaginatum), distinguished by its single tuft of white cotton. E. angustifolium has several flower spikes. Here, deep in the Sphagnum moss, you can find Sundew (Drosera rotundifolia). Their leaves are covered in sticky, reddish hairs that trap the insects that the plant needs for food in the nutrient-poor soil. Look for the oval-leaved Sundew (Drosera intermedia) which is less common. These tiny plants were known in my family as "Tennis Rackets and Cricket Bats ". On the stream margins and damp ground are Lousewort plants (Pedicularis sylvatica), with pink flowers, and feathery leaves. Bog Myrtle (Myrica gale) bushes grow here. Their pungent leaves were used to flavour beer and were said to produce hallucinations. The crushed leaves do keep the midges at bay. On the margins of streams and among wet rocks you can find Butterwort (Pinguicula vulgaris). This strange little plant has thick, bright green leaves and deep violet flowers floating on thin, wiry stems. Whilst you are among the rocks look for English Stonecrop (Sedum anglicum).

Boc Cotton

Climbing up to the sheilings, there are of course Buttercups (Ranunculus repens and R. acris), and Daisies (Bellis perennis). But if you search in the turf you will find Alpine Lady's Mantle (Alchemilla alpina) with its heads of many tiny green flowers, and umbrella shaped leaves each holding a rain drop if the weather is wet. The Heath Spotted Orchid (Dactylorhiza maculata) is fairly common on the hillsides. Look for its pale mauve, beautifully marked flowers. As you climb higher the flowers of this orchid will become white. In the shelter of the rocks grows the Hard Fern (Blechnum spicant) looking for all the world like green fish backbones. And if you look hard you will find the little Parsley Fern (Cryptogramma crispa) growing the crannies of old walls. It really does look like Flat-Leaved Parsley. In the gullies, where the sheep cannot clamber, you will see the remnants of the old woodlands; Rowan (Sorbus aucuparia), birch (Betula pubescens)and stunted oak trees (Quercus robur). Here are Wood Sanicle (Sanicula europeaus), Foxgloves (Digitalis purpurea), and Herb Robert (Geranium robertianum); this small member of the geranium family has bright pinkish mauve flowers and the palmate leaves are often reddish tinged. A number of thistles occur in the glen, of these three are easily spotted. Firstly, the Spear Thistle (Cirsium vulgare), a vigorous plant, with fearsomely spiny, dagger shaped leaves. Then there is the rarer and more stately Melancholy Thistle (Cirsium heterophyllum), only slightly prickly, with white, felted undersides to the leaves, and a single flower. And finally in the wetter places, the Marsh Thistle (Cirsium palustre) with clustered, dark purple flowers that are smaller than those of the other two thistles.

Towards the end of summer, mushrooms, (Agaricus campestris and its relatives) start to appear in the pasture land, and on the cow pats you will find a different sort of fungus called Dung Roundheads (Stropharia semiglobata). These are small toadstools, only two or three inches tall, with their yellowish-brown round heads perched on thin wiry stems. It is now that you will find flowers of the Bog Asphodel (Narthecium ossifragum) on the hillsides, like small greenish-yellow flames amongst the moorgrass.

GRASS
OF PARNASSUS

As the Autumn approaches, when the cows would be returned to the lower slopes, we can go with the farmer's wife as she travels through the glen to visit her relatives in Pennyghael. All three types of heather found on the island are flowering here; Ling (Calluna vulgaris), rich purple Bell Heather (Erica cinerea), and Cross Leaved Heath (Erica tetralix) with its tiny grey leaves and pinkish flowers. The Moor Grass has a patina of bronze now, and here and there you will see the mauve heads of Devil's Bit Scabious (Succisa pratensis). By the side of the road are the exquisite flowers of Grass of Parnassus (Parnassia palustris), chalk white with fine green lines on the petals. On beyond the little settlement at Craig, in the short grass are Autumn Hawkbit (Leontodon autumnalis) plants. Their dandelion-like leaves are deeply lobed, and the flowers, again resembling dandelions, grow on branched, wiry stems. Also you will find Mouse-ear Hawkweed, with oval leaves white-felted below, and single pale, lemon yellow flowers. And there is Fairy Flax (Linum catharticum). Only a fairy could make linen from threadlike stems that hold up the minute white

FAIRY
FLAX

flowers and dark green leaves. Worth finding for its delicate charm. As are the mysterious, dusky purple, upright spikes of the Field Gentian (Gentianella campestris). This plant is not common and only about two inches high where it has been heavily grazed. Here too you will see Waxcaps (Hygrocybe sp.). These fungi are common in wet Autumns. Some are a brilliant scarlet or yellow, others pallid white or, like the common Field Waxcap, pale orange. All have wax-like caps that glisten in the rain. There are other more sinister fungi too, these are Earth Tongues (Geoglossum sp). Black and about two inches tall, as their name suggests they are tongue shaped. The rowans are heavy with scarlet fruit, and there are bramble bushes with a good supply of blackberries. The Harebells (Campanula rotundifolia) are still in flower and blow in the wind from the sea that presages the gales to come.

Winter will come, and our farmer's wife will do well to return to Arinasliseig before the mists and snow make her journey perilous. The only patches of colour she will see on the barren, russet hills, are the occasional gorse bushes bravely showing their sweet-smelling yellow flowers even in the depths of winter - *When gorse is out of season, kissing is out of fashion* as the old saying goes.

WAX CAPS
AND
DUNG
ROUNDHEADS